If you haven't the vaguest idea what to do
When the doorbell goes PRRING; there's a parcel for you -
A mysterious package in paper and string
In which there's a box - a most puzzling thing -
Don't get yourself lost in the A-MAZE-ING views,
Just unravel the riddles and work out the clues.
And in times of confusion when nothing is plain,
Stick close to the page boy - engage your brain!

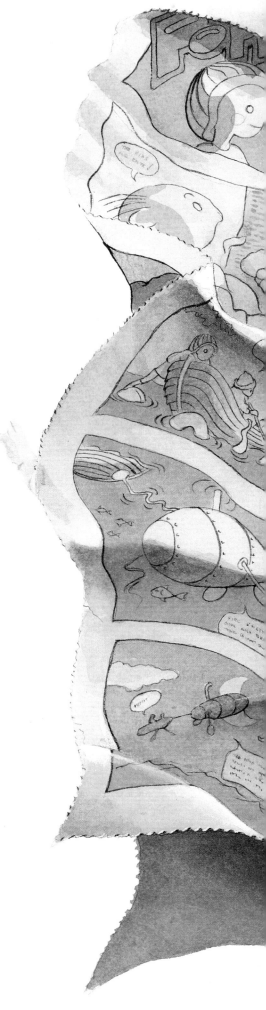

For the Right combination to open the box
Try the following rhyme and the secret unlocks.
Four numbers are SENT and Left as a clue,
It's the Right way you turn them, it's up to you.
Each number follows the one before -
Add them all up, what's Left? 34!

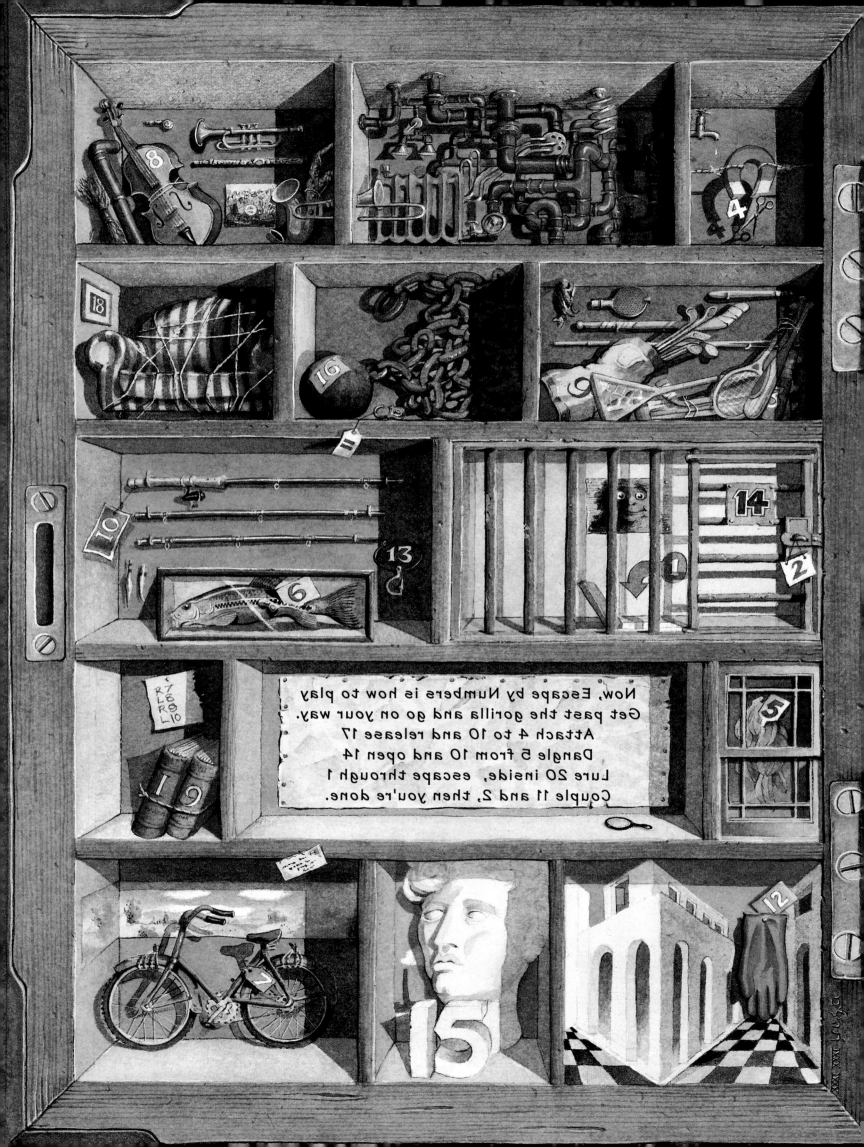

Escape from this scrape
- you will in a trice -
by using a coin
or counter and dice.

END

START

Land on a ladder,
Run up
- though it's steep -
Land on a puzzle,
Just solve it and leap

Six whole squares forward
But - shivers and shakes -
It's all the way back
If you land on the snakes.

To reach the OCEAN TOWER is the trick;
And there are several ways.
But can YOU do the arithmetic
To make it through the maze?

Now's not the time to make a fuss
Or you're dinner for an octopus!
If you're CRAFTY, there is no catch,
To getting safely down the hatch.
One fits, one twists, one holds up plugs,
One snips and one red herring tugs.
Go up four times, (you've been down five),
And then you might escape alive.

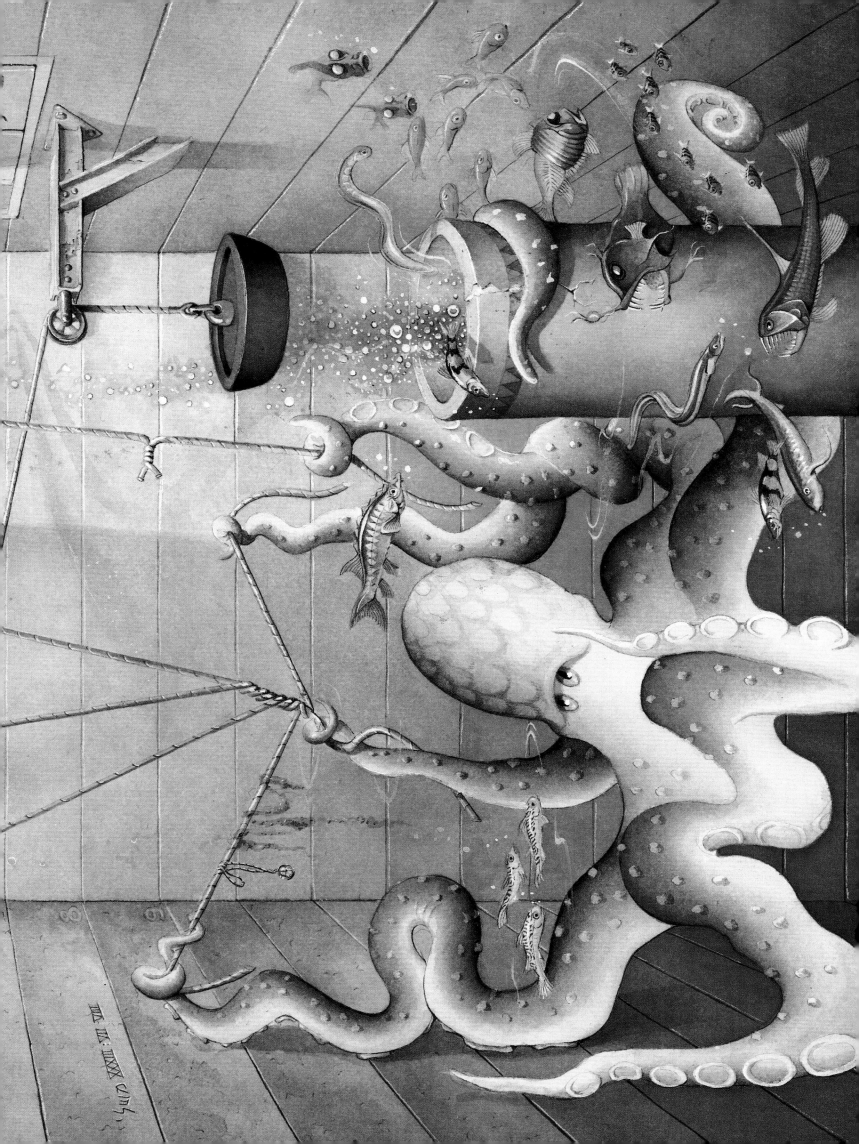

These blocks you see a Tower make,
Stack them up to cross the lake.
A jigsaw in a stone disguise
That you assemble with your eyes.
But not so fast, don't rush or race,
You must not fit a piece in place
Until you've found and solved for sure
The problem in the piece before.

The first step here is MAGNETISE
To clear the stairs, but recognise
There is an order to contrive.
The balls must roll down 1 to 5 -
Come from behind and PUSH them down,
Going now the long way round.

And as you get them underway
Beware what else comes into play -
The ratchet works the Dragon's Gate,
One drops you in it if you're late.
So what you need far more than pluck
Is speed and timing. Go! Good luck!

15000

10,000

2456

And now at last a simple game! The highest total is your aim. Use your dice and coin once more to get yourself a MONSTER score. Add up your own points as you go. Back and forwards with each throw. Get the REPLAY - if you dare. Read the instructions on each square.

1

2

3

3

1456

15000

OUT

OUT

REPLAY

OUT

To pass the vampire is your mission.
Put the levers in position.

So start with A, which goes above B
Which is level with C, though one above D
Which is two below A and one above E
Which couldn't be lower
- you've got him -
tee hee!

The Magic Sword

... now he lost his head.

Solve the sum to make it free
And he will vanish
immediately.

$3 \times 3 \times 3$

$10 \times 10 =$

$1 . ? ? ? = 9$

$= 6$

$= 7$

$= 10$

To pass the witch and break the spell
Make the potion, she hates the smell!

The map room's next, a   sticky trap,
So while the spider takes a nap
Use your wits and navigate
Your way by each co-ordinate.
Start at the steps, work on from there.
The secret door's a webless square.

At last, the greatest
mystery —
A box within a box
maybe?
And as the question's, When is tea?
Complete the jigsaw — find the key.

There is no need to be downhearted
To find you're back to where you started.
To find these things you missed before
Go back through the box once more.

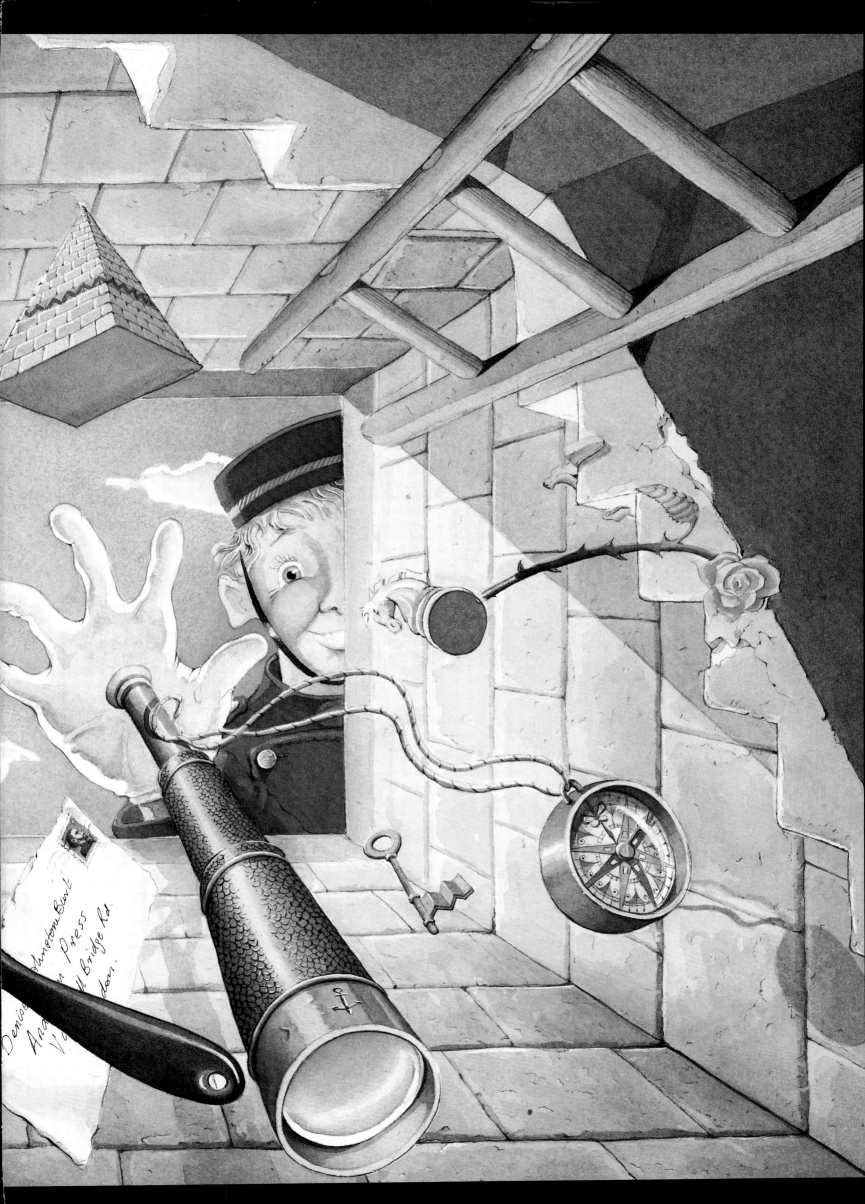

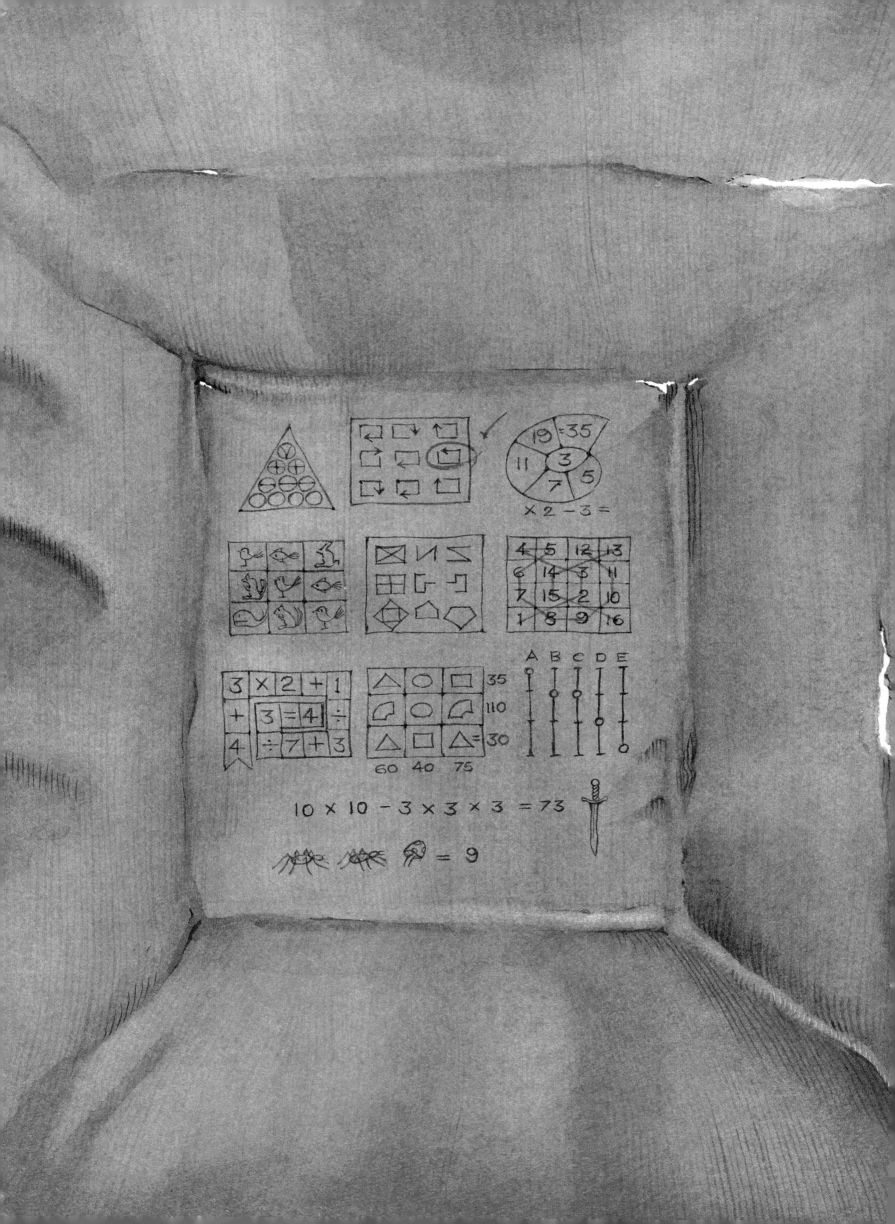